CH

1·2·3
I Can Make Prints!

Irene Luxbacher

KIDS CAN PRESS

A print is **ART** you make by pressing a thing you have painted onto a piece of paper to make a copy. It can look like something real or something you imagine. Let's make prints of insects …

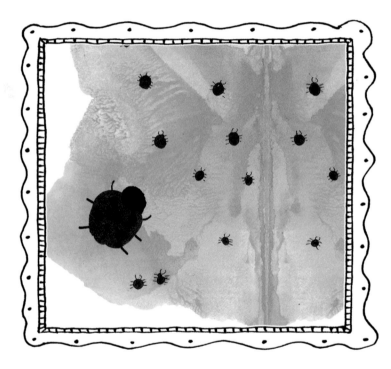

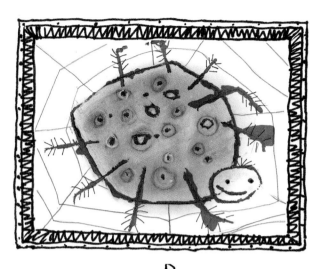

3

The things you use to make a print are called

MATERIALS.

- PLASTIC CONTAINERS OR ALUMINUM PIE PLATES (FOR MIXING YOUR PAINTS)

- LIQUID TEMPERA PAINTS OR ACRYLIC PAINTS

- PAPER

- BIG AND SMALL PAINT BRUSHES

- OLD NEWSPAPERS (TO PROTECT YOUR WORK SURFACE)

- SMOCK (TO PROTECT YOUR CLOTHES)

- SMALL FOAM PAINT ROLLER

- WHITE GLUE

4

• MODELING CLAY (LIKE PLAY DOUGH OR PLASTICINE)

• CLEAN FOAM TRAYS

• SCISSORS

• BIG AND SMALL SPONGES

• PIPE CLEANERS

• THICK CRAFT FOAM

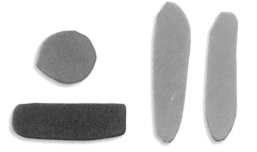

ARTIST'S SECRET:

Wiping your printing tools (the things you press into paint) with a clean, damp cloth after you've used them a few times will help you keep making nice, clear prints.

5

FINGER Prints

Get bzzz-y and use your THUMB and FINGERS to make some buzzing bumblebees!

1. Dab the pad of your thumb into a blob of yellow paint. Press your thumb onto your paper. Repeat until you fill your paper with lots of bumblebee bodies. Let the paint dry.

2. Dab the tip of your baby finger into a blob of black paint. Press your baby finger near the end of a bumblebee to make its head. Repeat for all your bees. Let the paint dry.

3. Dab the tip of another clean finger into a blob of gray or white paint. Press your finger onto a bumblebee twice to give it two wings. Repeat for all your bees. Let the paint dry.

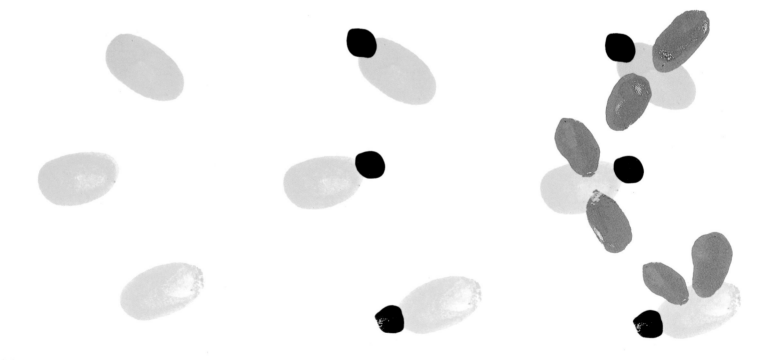

BUZZ! Very Busy Bees!

Once your prints are dry, use a small paintbrush and black paint to add stripes to your bumblebees. Draw their legs and antennae using a thin-tipped black marker. And why are the bees so busy? Add a few colorful flowers for your bees to buzz around using paint, chalk or markers.

Dipping something like your finger or a sponge into paint and pressing it onto paper to make a print is called STAMPING.

7

PRESSED-ON Pattern

Use painted sponges to make a pattern that looks like a caterpillar
CREEPING and CRAWLING across your page!

1. Dab a large sponge into a blob of brightly colored paint.
Gently press the sponge onto your paper. Dab a smaller sponge
into a blob of a different-colored paint. Gently press the sponge
onto your paper, right next to the first print.

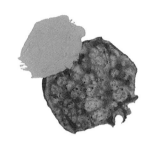

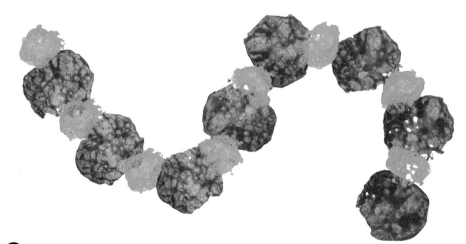

2. Repeat Step 1 over and
over until you fill the page with a
long, curving caterpillar's body.
Let the paint dry.

3. Bend the tip of a pipe
cleaner to make an "L." Dab the
short end of the pipe cleaner into
a blob of black paint. Gently
press the pipe cleaner along your
caterpillar's body to make lots of
fuzzy legs. Let dry.

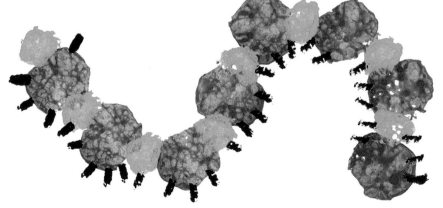

ZOOM!
A Crazy Caterpillar!

Use a small paintbrush and paint to give your caterpillar a few colorful stripes and spots, antennae and a face. Dip your baby finger in paint to make fingerprints that look like scurrying feet!

A **PATTERN** is a design that is repeated. By putting a large print next to a small print over and over for the caterpillar's body, you made a pattern.

In the FOLD

Fold a painted piece of paper in half to make a print
of a leaf and ladybugs that will be TWICE as NICE!

1. Add a little water to some green paint so it's a bit runny. Use a big paintbrush to drop a blob of paint in the middle of your paper. Fold the paper in half, gently squishing the paint in the fold. Smooth the paper with your hands. Carefully open the paper and let your leaf print dry.

2. Clean your brush and drop a smaller blob of red paint onto the edge of your leaf print. Fold the paper again, gently squishing the blob of paint. Carefully open the paper and let your ladybug prints dry.

3. Use a small paintbrush to add a small blob of black paint to the tip of one ladybug for a head. Add a few tiny black spots to the ladybug's body. Fold the paper again, gently squishing the blobs of paint. Carefully open the paper and let dry.

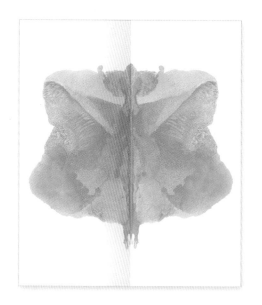

SHHH ... Two Sleepy Ladybugs!

Add legs to your ladybugs with more black paint. Then try filling your leaf with tiny dark green dots of paint so your ladybugs have lots of aphids to count! Give your aphids lots of little legs of their own with a thin-tipped black marker.

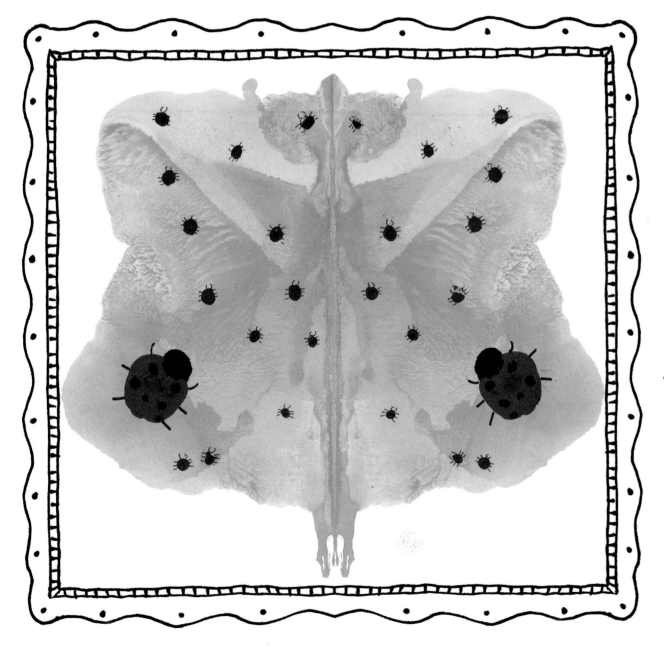

When a picture is even or equal on both sides, it has **SYMMETRY** (say SIM-meh-tree).

What a RELIEF

By gluing foam shapes onto a piece of thick cardboard, you can make a print of a dragonfly that really STANDS OUT!

1. Carefully cut a circle, a rectangle and four long ovals out of thick craft foam.

2. Make your shapes into a dragonfly by putting two ovals on each side of the rectangle. Then put the circle at the top of the rectangle. Spread some white glue on the shapes and carefully press a piece of cardboard on top. Let the glue dry for a few hours.

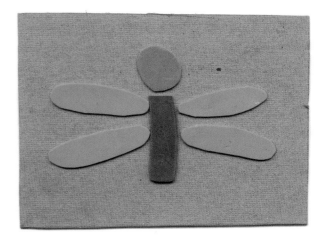

3. Use a paintbrush to paint the foam dragonfly one color or a few colors. Turn the cardboard over and press your dragonfly firmly onto a piece of paper.

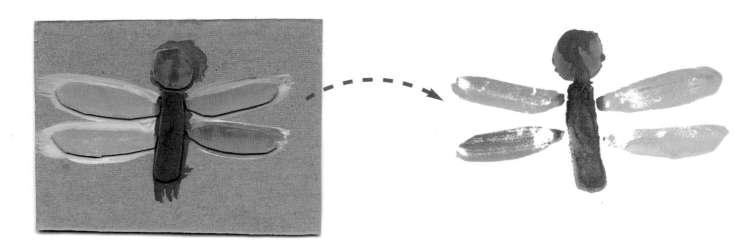

WHRRR!
Dancing Dragonflies!

Press your dragonfly onto the paper again and again until the prints are too faded to see. Carefully clean it with a damp cloth so you can use a new color or colors to fill the paper with dozens more dragonflies. When the prints are dry, give your dragonflies faces, legs, stripes and spots using markers and paint.

The painted foam shapes sticking up from the cardboard leave behind a print of a dragonfly on the paper. This is called a RELIEF PRINT.

DIGGING In

Carve some DEEP GROOVES into a foam tray to make a print that looks like the twisting, turning tunnels of an anthill.

1. Cut off the curved edges of a clean foam tray so it lies nice and flat. Then use a pencil to draw lots of curving lines into the tray. Press hard to make deep grooves (but not holes) in the foam.

2. Use a paint roller to lightly cover the foam tray in brown paint. Make sure you can still see the grooves you made for the ant tunnels.

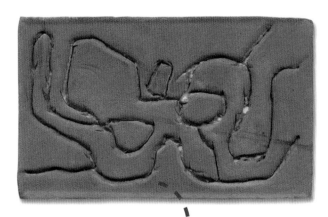

3. Quickly flip the painted side of the foam tray onto a sheet of paper. Press the tray down with both of your hands. Carefully lift up the tray, trying not to smudge the print of the ant tunnels you have made. Let dry.

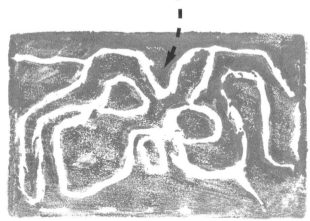

UH-OH!
An Underground Anthill!

If you want to, use a paintbrush to fill in the parts of your anthill that didn't get covered with enough brown paint. Let the paint dry. Add a sky above your anthill with blue chalk or paint. Use a black marker or a pen to draw lots of busy ants crawling through the tunnels.

The grooves you made in the foam are the unpainted parts of your print. This is called a BLOCK PRINT.

Get into the GROOVE

You never know what prints you'll unearth when you play with modeling clay! Try it and see with this super spider print.

1. Flatten out a lump of clay so it's about as thick as your thumb. Wrap a piece of aluminum foil around the clay. Draw a spider in the foil-covered clay using a pencil. Press hard enough to make nice deep grooves.

2. Paint over the spider using a paintbrush and one of your favorite colors of paint. Use a damp cloth to carefully wipe off the foil so that the paint is only in the grooves of the clay.

3. Quickly flip the painted side of the foil-covered clay onto a sheet of paper. Press it down with both of your hands. Gently peel your clay away from the paper. Let the print dry.

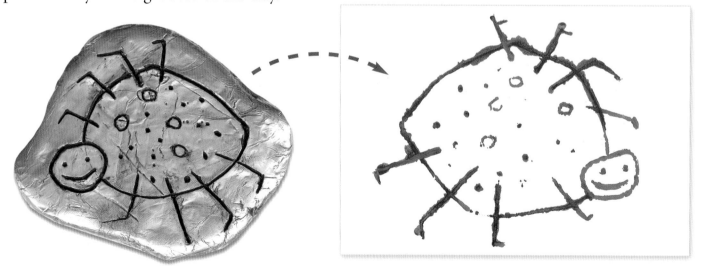

SILLY!
A Spinning Spider!

Draw a web spun by your spider with a pencil or thin-tipped marker. Use markers, paint or chalk to add colorful spots and patterns to your spider's body.

The grooves you made in the clay are the painted parts of your print. This is called an INTAGLIO PRINT (say in-TAG-lee-o).

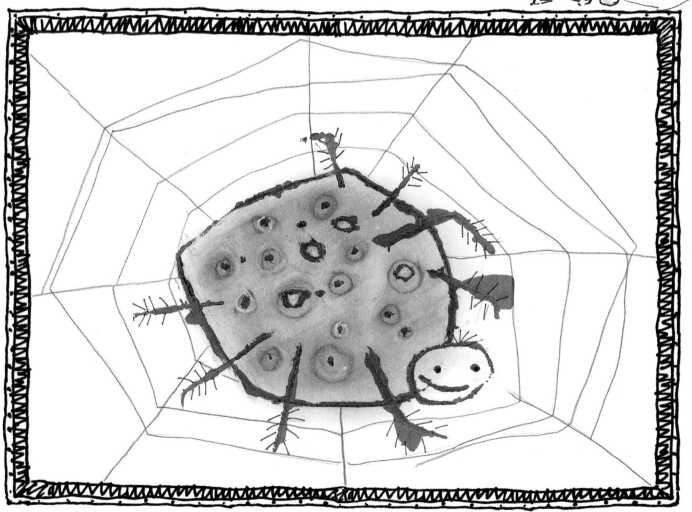

17

ONE OF A KIND

Imagine the one-of-a-kind butterfly you might make
if you put ALL your favorite printing ideas TOGETHER.

HEAD AND BODY

Dip your thumb into some black paint and make a line of thumbprints
down the middle of the paper. This is the butterfly's body. Dip your
other thumb into another color of paint and make two prints at the top
for a head. Let dry.

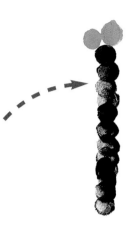

FRONT WINGS

Use a big brush to drop a big, watery blob of
brightly colored paint on one side of the
body. Fold your paper in half along the body,
gently squishing the paint. Carefully open the
paper and let your butterfly's front wings dry.

BACK WINGS

Carefully cut a round wing out of a clean foam
tray. Decorate the wing by carving in some deep
grooves with a pencil. Use a paint roller to lightly
cover the wing with some brightly colored paint
and press it below one of the front wings.
Repeat on the other side. Let dry.

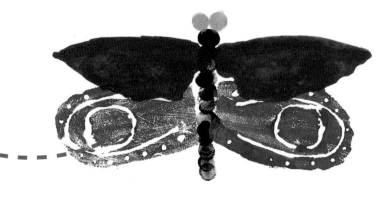

ANTENNAE

Cut out a piece of craft foam that looks like a skinny antenna. Glue the foam onto a piece of cardboard and let it dry. Paint the foam with some colorful paint and press it on top of your bug's head twice, to make two antennae prints.

WING PATTERNS

Dip a large sponge in some colorful paint and gently press it onto your butterfly's wings. Dip a small sponge into another color of paint and gently press it next to your first print. Repeat this step as many times as you like to make a printed pattern.

WING DESIGNS

Use a pencil to carve a design into a flattened piece of modeling clay that has been wrapped in aluminum foil. Brush some colorful paint over the design. Use a damp cloth to carefully wipe the extra paint off the clay. Press the clay onto your butterfly's wings as many times as you like.

OH MY!
A Rare and Beautiful Butterfly!

Use more fingerprints to add eyes and bright spots of color to your butterfly. Dip the bent end of a pipecleaner in paint and press it next to the butterfly's body to make fuzzy legs.

Your rare butterfly is a **MONOPRINT**. A monoprint uses more than one technique at a time and is different each time you make it.

Note to PARENTS and TEACHERS

We chose insects as a fun theme to explore some basic printmaking techniques, but there are lots of other topics or themes you can use to inspire your young artist. Here are a few ideas to get you started:

• Make a print of a brightly colored bird. Carve some puffy clouds into a foam tray to print a big, blue sky on a sheet of paper (see Digging In, page 14). Make some colorful feathers by pressing a small sponge dipped in paint to make overlapping prints (see Pressed-on Pattern, page 8). Give your feathered friend a fingerprint beak and eyes (see Finger Prints, page 6).

• Or follow the trail of your favorite animals. Make some bird tracks by dipping the bent ends of pipe cleaners into paint and stamping them on your page (see Pressed-on Pattern, page 8). Make bear tracks by pressing the painted palms of your hands on your page and using your fingerprints for bear toes (see Finger Prints, page 6). Try making a huge dinosaur track by pressing a blob of paint between the fold of a piece of paper (see In the Fold, page 10). Cut out craft foam triangles and glue them to a piece of cardboard to give your dinosaur footprint some claws (see What a Relief, page 12).

Tips to ensure a GOOD PRINTMAKING EXPERIENCE every time:

1. Use inexpensive materials and make sure your young artist's clothes and the work area are protected. This way it's all about the fun, not the waste and the mess.

2. Focus on the process rather than the end product. Make sure your young artist is relaxed and having fun with the information instead of expecting perfection every time.

3. Remind your young artist that mistakes are an artist's best friend. The most interesting printmaking ideas and results are often discovered by mistake.

PRINTMAKING Words

BLOCK PRINT
page 15

MONOPRINT
page 20

RELIEF PRINT
page 13

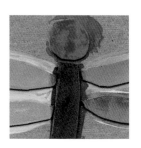

INTAGLIO PRINT
page 17

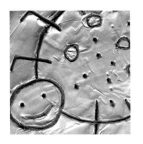

PATTERN
page 9

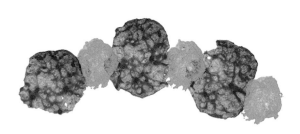

STAMPING
page 7

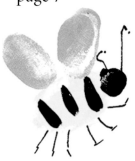

MATERIALS
page 4

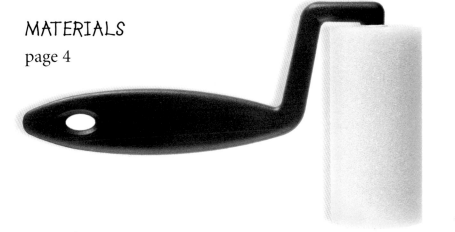

SYMMETRY
page 11

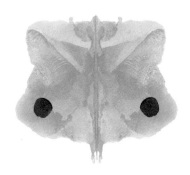

FOR ELIJAH AND NOAH

Special thanks to Stacey Roderick and Karen Powers. This book would not have been possible without their amazing talents and insights.

Text and illustrations © 2008 Irene Luxbacher

Kids Can Press acknowledges the financial support of the Government of Ontario, through the Ontario Media Development Corporation's Ontario Book Initiative, and the Government of Canada, through the BPIDP, for our publishing activity.

Published in Canada by
Kids Can Press Ltd.
29 Birch Avenue
Toronto, ON M4V 1E2

Published in the U.S. by
Kids Can Press Ltd.
2250 Military Road
Tonawanda, NY 14150

www.kidscanpress.com

Kids Can Press is a *Corus*™ Entertainment company

Edited by Stacey Roderick
Designed by Karen Powers

Photos on pages 4–5: Ray Boudreau
(except scissors: © iStockphoto.com/Mark Yuill and sponges © iStockphoto.com/Bill Noll)
Printed and bound in Singapore

The hardcover edition of this book is smyth sewn casebound. The paperback edition of this book is limp sewn with a drawn-on cover.

CM 08 0 9 8 7 6 5 4 3 2 1
CM PA 08 0 9 8 7 6 5 4 3 2 1

Library and Archives Canada Cataloguing in Publication

Luxbacher, Irene, 1970–
     123 I can make prints! / Irene Luxbacher.

(Starting art)
ISBN 978-1-55453-040-3 (bound)
ISBN 978-1-55453-153-0 (pbk.)

1. Prints—Technique—Juvenile literature. I. Title.
II. Title: One, two, three I can make prints!
III. Series: Luxbacher, Irene, 1970– Starting art.

NE860.L89 2008   j760.28   C2007-902726-1